RECREATIONAL DRONES

by Matt Chandler

CAPSTONE PRESS
a capstone imprint

Edge Books are published by Capstone Press,
1710 Roe Crest Drive, North Mankato, Minnesota 56003
www.mycapstone.com

Library of Congress Cataloging-in-Publication Data
Library of Congress Cataloging-in-Publication data is available on the Library of
Congress website.

ISBN: 978-1-5157-3766-7 (library binding)
ISBN: 978-1-5157-3770-4 (paperback)
ISBN: 978-1-5157-3794-0 (eBook PDF)

Editorial Credits
Carrie Sheely, editor; Steve Mead, designer; Tracey Engel, media researcher;
Katy LaVigne, production specialist

Photo Credits
123RF: modfos, 24; Alamy: Maurice Savage, 18, ZUMA Press, Inc., 27; AP Images: Peter
Thomson/La Crosse Tribune, 25, Kamran Jebreili, 5; Getty Images: Ethan Miller/Staff, 6–7,
Neo Chee Wei/Contributor, 14; iStockphoto: Franck-Boston, 16–17; Newscom: CHARLES
PLATIAU/REUTERS, 20–21, CHINE NOUVELLE/SIPA/1509101149, 29; Shutterstock: Andis
Rea, Design Element, Brothers Good, Cover and Interior Design Element, Chesky, Design
Element, DamienGeso, Design Element, Fineart1, 13, Kolonkok, Design Element, Konstantin
Ustinov, Design Element, LiliGraphie, Cover Background, Nik Merkulov, Cover and Interior
Design Element, Pagina, Design Element, ProstoSvet, Front and Back Cover, robuart,
Design Element, seregalsv, 8–9, SunnyStock, 11, Vjom, Cover and Interior Design Element;
SuperStock: Alf Jönsson/imageBROKER, 23

Printed and bound in China.
007890

TABLE OF CONTENTS

CHAPTER 1

Drone Flying Fun

Bonney Field in Sacramento, California, is usually home to soccer tournaments. But in the summer of 2015 during the state fair, the field was transformed into a flight zone. More than 100 drone pilots took part in the Fat Shark U.S. National Drone Racing Championships. At first glance, it might have looked like the seated racers were just relaxing with friends. But upon a closer look, their goggles and slight, quick hand movements would have told a different story. These racers were locked in fierce competition while twisting their drones through a challenging course. In the end, Australian pilot Chad Nowak became the first U.S. national champion.

Drones have been around for nearly 100 years. The first **recreational** drones were a **novelty** for many years. In the 1930s they drew attention from just a small group of enthusiasts. Unlike today's battery-operated models, early drones ran on gasoline. These bulky airplanes often had wingspans of more than 10 feet (3 meters).

 recreational—done for enjoyment, usually in people's spare time

novelty—something new, interesting, and unusual

Today more than 400,000 recreational drones are in use in the United States. Hundreds of thousands more fly worldwide. Events like the National Drone Racing Championships draw hundreds of competitors. After the competitions are over, thousands of people might view online videos of the events.

FACT

Competitors at major drone races can win huge cash prizes. In 2016 British teenager Luke Bannister piloted a drone at the World Drone Prix in Dubai, United Arab Emirates. He won the $250,000 grand prize.

Luke Bannister

CHAPTER 2

Choosing a Drone

Drones that fly are also called unmanned aerial vehicles (UAVs). All UAVs share some features. A pilot on the ground operates a UAV using a **remote control** device. Some UAVs also can fly on a pre-programmed flight path. Beyond that, each UAV has its own unique features and capabilities. Buyers choose recreational drones based on their own needs and preferences.

Parrot's Disco fixed-wing drone can fly about 50 miles (80 km) per hour.

Drones can have **rotors** or fixed wings. Quadcopters are one of the most common types of rotor drones. They have four rotors. Other recreational drones have six or eight rotors. The biggest difference in the number of rotors is the amount of **thrust** the drone can generate.

Fixed-wing drones don't have rotors. They look like small airplanes. These drones usually have a longer battery life than rotor drones do.

Some drones are even multi-purpose. Parrot's Hydrofoil drone can fly in the air. But it can also ride on the surface of the water. As a watercraft, it reaches a top speed of 6 miles (10 kilometers) per hour.

FACT

Axis Drones' Aerius mini-drone is so small it fits on the tip of a finger.

remote control—a device used to control machines from a distance

rotor—a set of rotating blades that lifts an aircraft off the ground

thrust—the force that moves a vehicle

DRONES FOR EVERY EXPERIENCE LEVEL

With so many choices available, buying a drone is no simple task. A beginner pilot may want an inexpensive drone that is easier to replace when it crashes. Beginners can buy a basic drone for as little as $25.

As pilots get better at flying, they can upgrade to more advanced flying machines. An experienced pilot may choose an octocopter. This type of drone has eight arms that each operate on an individual motor. Pilots can often attach large cameras to these strong drones.

DRONES FOR SPECIFIC PURPOSES

Before buying, hobbyists should consider how they will use the drone. Racers need a small drone with a lot of power, such as the OFM Seeker 450 V2 quadcopter. This drone can reach a top speed of 62 miles (100 km) per hour. It is one of the fastest racing drones on the market today. Some racers have drones with carbon fiber frames. Carbon fiber is lightweight yet strong.

FACT

If one or two engines fail on an octocopter, the pilot can still land the drone with the remaining engines.

 An octocopter flies through the air holding a large camera.

DRONES FOR PHOTOGRAPHY

The ability to take stunning videos and photos is a main attraction for many drone enthusiasts. Drone cameras allow hobbyists to capture overhead shots of mountainous regions, forests, and other areas. Buyers interested in photography should consider the quality of a drone's cameras. The quality of cameras on recreational drones varies. Some basic cameras have 2-**megapixel resolution**, while advanced cameras often have at least 10-megapixel resolution. Most drones also have **high-definition** (HD) video cameras.

Professional photographers often use the Phantom 3. This drone snaps 12-megapixel still photos. A wide-angle lens captures a large area to the sides. The drone also has image stabilization to reduce blurring. A control lets the pilot easily hover to take images.

FACT

In 2016 the Federal Aviation Administration (FAA) updated its rules for those who want to fly drones for business use in the United States. Pilots of drones weighing from 0.55 to 55 pounds (250 grams to 25 kilograms) must be at least 16 years old. They also need to complete training and get a certificate. These pilots also need to follow all of the FAA's other drone rules.

The DJI Phantom 3 can stay in the air about 20 minutes before needing to be recharged.

megapixel—one million pixels; a pixel is a very small dot that makes up a picture on a TV screen, computer monitor, or other digital device

resolution—the ability of a device to show an image clearly and with a lot of detail

high-definition—having a high clarity of visual presentation; cameras labeled as HD meet certain resolution and other standards

CRASH CONSIDERATIONS

Drones are built to be lightweight and fast. However, these qualities also make drones vulnerable. Most popular recreational drones won't survive a crash from hundreds of feet in the air. Weather can easily cause a drone to crash. Even a light gust of wind can send a tiny drone off course. When purchasing a drone, buyers need to consider how well the drone will stand up to crashes.

Some manufacturers sell crash kits. These kits can come with everything from replacement propellers to a new body cover for the drone. Crash kits allow many repairs to be made in the field at a minimal cost.

Owners of more expensive drones may buy drone **insurance**. The insurance can cover some of the costs resulting from a crash.

FACT

The small Walkera QR Infra X Smart drone was the first to have a crash-avoidance system. If an object is nearby, it will automatically fly in the opposite direction.

 insurance—an agreement in which a person makes regular payments to a company and the company promises to pay money if the item insured is damaged or lost

Crashes can easily damage fragile parts such as propellers. Replacement propellers and other parts can be helpful to have on hand.

DIY DRONES

With so many types of drones available, there is a drone that fits the needs of almost every buyer. But some people want the challenge of building their own **custom** drones. These drone enthusiasts either use drone kits or build drones from scratch. Basic kits have everything needed to build a drone for less than $100.

A man gets ready to fly his homemade drone in a park in Singapore.

To build a drone from scratch, all the parts must be purchased individually. Building a custom drone in this way isn't for beginners. Like any complex machine, building a drone takes a lot of knowledge and patience. An understanding of **aerodynamics** is critical. The way a builder shapes a drone and positions the rotors will determine its success in flight. Knowledge of small-engine design can help hobbyists build their own engines. Experience with **robotics** can lead to even more features. Imagine a drone with a robotic arm that can land and grab you a snack!

Experts say the advantage to building a drone is having a better understanding of how it works. Drones can be tricky to fly, and many inexperienced operators crash their drones. Building your own drone can lead to better piloting skills.

custom—specially done or made

aerodynamics—the ability of something to move easily and quickly through the air

robotics—field that deals with the design, construction, and operation of robots

CHAPTER 3

Get Behind the Controls

Once you have a drone, it's time for the most exciting part—getting behind the controls! Children as young as 7 can learn to fly a simple drone.

The handheld controller is the pilot's connection to the drone. Just like a video game controller, most recreational drone controllers have two joysticks. These are used to control the **pitch**, **yaw**, throttle, and **roll** of the drone. The throttle determines how fast the drone travels. Once it is airborne, the pilot must maintain the drone's height in the air while controlling the other elements.

One of the most important maneuvers for a pilot to master is the roll. Many drone crashes happen when a pilot flies the drone into an object such as a building or tree. A roll can redirect the drone and avoid a crash.

pitch—to turn on an axis so that the forward end rises or falls in relation to the other end

yaw—movement of an aircraft to the left or right

roll—movement of an aircraft in a circular motion to the left or right

Many drones have a screen on the controller. This lets pilots see the view from the drone's camera.

KNOW THE RULES

Before you fly, there are some rules to know. The FAA sets drone rules in the United States. Drones more than 0.55 pound (250 g) and less than 55 pounds (25 kg) flown outdoors need to be registered. The person registering must be at least 13 years old.

Some pilots have reported drones flying within 100 feet (30 meters) of their planes. This close distance can lead to a collision.

KEEPING OTHERS SAFE

By following rules, you help protect others. A recreational drone can weigh as much as 55 pounds (25 kg). That's enough to cause a commercial airliner to crash under the right conditions if the two aircraft collide. In 2014 U.S. pilots reported more than 230 sightings of recreational drones. In 2015 that number jumped to almost 600 sightings in a six-month period.

Drone pilots also must follow the FAA's in-flight rules. Pilots can fly no higher than 400 feet (122 m) in the air. They cannot interfere with manned aircraft. Pilots must keep drones beyond 5 miles (8 km) of an airport unless they have permission. Pilots cannot fly over air shows or major sporting events without permission. They must keep drones within sight at all times. This is known as maintaining a visual line of sight.

CHAPTER 4

RECREATIONAL DRONE USES

From racing to photography, the uses of recreational drones are many. Some people like to post "selfies" on social media to share with their friends. Thanks to drones, there is a new type of photo gaining popularity—the "dronie." To make one, fly your drone and snap a shot of yourself. Imagine how different you might look from 50 feet (15 m) above the ground!

FIGHTING DRONES

Though it's still rare, some pilots take part in drone combat. The rules are simple: the last drone flying wins. Battle rules allow bumping the opponent's drone in an attempt to make it crash. Drone fights can sharpen the skills of pilots. To escape an attack drone, a pilot might need to make several quick dives or turns. A combat drone group called Game of Drones holds events in the San Francisco area that draw hundreds of spectators.

FACT

Hundreds of drone clubs operate around the world. By joining a club, pilots can share their hobby with others and learn more about drones.

Drone enthusiasts gather at the Intergalactic Meeting of Phantom's Pilots in Paris, France, in 2014.

RACING DRONES

As drones have become more popular, drone racing has become more organized. For most races, competitors race around a marked course for a certain number of laps. The racer with the fastest time wins. Classes are often divided up based on the type of drone being flown. Other races are based on a points system. Racers earn points for finishing each **heat** under a set amount of time. The racer with the most points after a certain number of heats wins. Racers often need to qualify for championship events by winning in smaller events.

DRONE RACING LEAGUE

The Drone Racing League is a large competitive racing group that draws pilots from around the world. The league holds events throughout the United States. Pilots are ranked nationally in standings. In 2016 the group held a race inside Sun Life Stadium in Miami, Florida. The stadium is home to the NFL's Miami Dolphins.

 heat—a single round of a contest

Thanks to first-person-view (FPV) flying, racers can feel as though they are in the cockpit of the drone. The drone camera relays real-time video back to a pair of goggles worn by the pilot.

FACT

Many racers add neon lights to their racing drones. This makes the drones more visible for race spectators.

A racer uses FPV goggles to fly his drone.

PUTTING DRONES TO WORK

Recreational drones are made to fly for fun. But that doesn't mean they can't be used for purposeful work. If a homeowner has a leak in the attic, he or she may have to climb to the roof to inspect the damage. This can be dangerous. Instead, the homeowner can fly a drone over the house and photograph the roof. The owner can then instantly see the damage without ever leaving the ground.

Gardeners can use drones to inspect their gardens and identify areas that need attention. This can be especially helpful in rural areas where a garden or orchard may be acres away.

Drones can help workers and homeowners safely inspect rooftops.

DRONES FOR POLICE USE

You might be used to seeing police officers chasing suspects on TV. But imagine a suspect being chased by a drone! Law enforcement agencies are just one of many groups using recreational drones for business use. Police in Mesa County, Colorado, were some of the first officers to use drones in the United States. The drones have logged more than 300 hours of flight time and have been on more than 80 missions. Police use the drones to track suspects, re-create crime scenes, and other jobs.

CHAPTER 5

THE FUTURE OF RECREATIONAL DRONES

Recreational drone use shows no signs of slowing down. The FAA predicts that by 2020 there will be 4.3 million recreational drones in the United States alone. Add to that several million commercial drones and the skies will be crowded. With this increase, new laws are likely to come. These laws can help protect people from injury and help ensure people's privacy.

In recent years drone manufacturers have partnered to help promote drone use and fair laws for them. In 2016 some leading drone manufacturers formed the Drone Manufacturers Alliance. Members of the group include DJI, 3D Robotics, GoPro, and Parrot. The group wants to promote laws that allow safe use of drones. They also want to promote creative design in drone manufacturing.

CHECKING LOCAL LAWS

Drone owners need to know laws specific to where they are flying. Both national and local laws may change depending on the area. For example, the FAA has stricter guidelines in the Washington, D.C., area for national defense reasons. In 2015 a recreational drone user was flying a drone at night. He lost control of the quadcopter. He knew the drone would soon run out of battery life. He thought it would crash nearby, so he didn't go to look for it right away. But the next day he learned it had crashed at the White House. Despite his mistake, he was not charged with a crime.

Drone manufacturers will continue to push the limits with new drone technology and capabilities. Object avoidance is one area of drone technology manufacturers are trying to improve. In 2016 two researchers at Stanford University in California made a drone that can dodge the quick jabs of a fencing sword. Improvements in this area can help drones travel more safely. In contrast, the Gimball rescue drone is designed to survive bumping into objects. This rescue drone won the Drones for Good international competition in 2015. Its hardy design would allow it to bounce off of objects while searching for victims in wilderness areas.

The use of cutting-edge technology will increase the options from which drone buyers have to choose. These advancements will also help expand the types of jobs drones can do. From inspections in factories to making life-saving deliveries, the possibilities for drones seem endless.

A woman displays the Gimball drone at a World Economic Forum meeting in China in 2015.

FACT

In 2015 the first International Drone Day events were held. Organizers formed the events to help promote the benefits of drone use.

GLOSSARY

aerodynamics (air-oh-dy-NA-miks)—the ability of something to move easily and quickly through the air

custom (KUHS-tuhm)—specially done or made

high definition (HY de-fuh-NI-shuhn)—having a high clarity of visual presentation; cameras labeled as HD meet a certain resolution standard and other requirements

heat (HEET)—a single round of a contest

insurance (in-SHUR-uhnss)—an agreement in which a person makes regular payments to a company and the company promises to pay money if the item insured is damaged or lost

megapixel (ME-guh-pik-sul)—one million pixels; a pixel is a very small dot that makes up a picture on a TV screen, computer monitor, or other digital device

novelty (NAH-vul-tee)—something new, interesting, and unusual

pitch (PICH)—to turn on an axis so that the forward end rises or falls in relation to the other end

recreational (re-kree-AY-shu-nul)—done for enjoyment, usually in people's spare time

remote control (ri-MOHT kuhn-TROHL)—a device used to control machines from a distance

resolution (re-zuh-LOO-shuhn)—the ability of a device to show an image clearly and with a lot of detail

robotics (ro-BOT-iks)—field that deals with the design, construction, and operation of robots

roll (ROL)—movement of an aircraft in a circular motion to the left or right

rotor (ROH-tur)—a set of rotating blades that lifts an aircraft off the ground

thrust (THRUST)—the force that moves a vehicle

yaw (YAW)—movement of an aircraft to the left or right

READ MORE

Brook, Henry. *Drones.* London, England: Usborne Books, 2016.

Collard, Sneed. *Technology Forces: Drones and War Machines.* New York: Rourke Educational Media, 2013.

Faust, Daniel. *Drones: Eyes in the Skies.* New York: PowerKids Press, 2016.

Scholastic. *Drones: From Insect Spy Drones to Bomber Drones.* New York: Scholastic, 2014.

INTERNET SITES

FactHound offers a safe, fun way to find Internet sites related to this book. All of the sites on FactHound have been researched by our staff.

Here's all you do:

Visit *www.facthound.com*

Type in this code: 9781515737667

Check out projects, games and lots more at
www.capstonekids.com

INDEX